Learn to Look BEYOND THE Storm

Learn to Look BEYOND THE Storm

Inspirational Poems For Your Journey

BELINDA A. L. BLAND

Xulon Press

Xulon Press
2301 Lucien Way #415
Maitland, FL 32751
407.339.4217
www.xulonpress.com

© 2020 by BELINDA A. L. BLAND

All rights reserved solely by the author. The author guarantees all contents are original and do not infringe upon the legal rights of any other person or work. No part of this book may be reproduced in any form without the permission of the author. The views expressed in this book are not necessarily those of the publisher.

Unless otherwise indicated, Scripture quotations taken from The Message (MSG). Copyright © 1993, 1994, 1995, 1996, 2000, 2001, 2002. Used by permission of NavPress Publishing Group. Used by permission. All rights reserved.

Printed in the United States of America.

ISBN-13: 978-1-6305-0629-2

TABLE OF CONTENTS

INTRODUCTION vii
DEDICATIONS. xi
ACKNOWLEDGEMENTS xiii

THE PROMISE REVEALED 1
YOU ARE MY VESSEL 3
THANK GOD FOR THE STORM 5
EARLY IN THE MORNING, I RISE 8
WHERE ARE YOU, LORD 11
A BLESSING IN DUE TIME 17
YOU'RE LOOKING FOR A MIRACLE 19
SPEAK TO YOUR MOUNTAIN –
   IT'S ONLY A DELAY 21
TODAY SOMEONE ASKED 24
MY ANEW 26
LEARN TO LOOK BEYOND THE STORM 29
PICTURES OF OUR JOURNEY 33
ABOUT THE AUTHOR. 51
COMING SOON! 53

INTRODUCTION

We have seen so often the design of God's natural storm with our very own eyes. Have you ever really thought about a thunderstorm? We see rain and lightning, and feel the wind. But at the end of the storm, the sun shines again and sometimes He places a beautiful rainbow in the sky. We have even witnessed double rainbows at times.

Just like a natural storm, we have our spiritual storms. And just as storms in this world come in many ways and intensities and have different impacts on our lives, so do our storms in the spiritual part of our lives. My husband has often stated before, "Some of us are in a storm right now, some of us are coming out of a storm, and some of us are about to go into a storm." No matter who you are, storms are a part of life, and we are destined to face them. But I want to encourage you to look for God in the midst of your storm, get out of the boat, and walk on water. He is there to help you through!

I pray that through the ministering of the Holy Spirit, you will come to understand the reason for the storms in your life and out of obedience, God will reveal the promises He has waiting for you. The storms of life, they don't come to destroy you; they come to strengthen you and make you better. Every experience we go through is a divine plan of God.

After each poem is a journaling opportunity where you can think on the poem's theme and write how it relates to your life. As you prepare to go further in this book of poems, remember this: storms are a way of preparation for a great move of God in your life, for the results of the storm will be change, strength, greatness, greater faith, and success. Storms cause us to trust ourselves less and God more. In everyone's rainy days, there are clouds. My cloud when I wrote this book of poems in 2002 was loneliness and a desire to marry. At the age of forty years and having never married, with no children, I had a great desire to be married and have children. God has a way of personalizing your storms just for you to get out of you what He desires. But I learned to look beyond what I saw as a storm, and God blessed me.

A love story was written by Heaven in 2003 when I married. God gave me a granddaughter through my marriage, whom we raised as our own. Now, married and having gained strength from the storms of life, I was able to face my husband's diagnosis of Multiple Sclerosis (MS) head on when he was diagnosed nine years into our marriage. I was now challenged with the vow that I gave before God, "in sickness and in health." Because of these challenges I have endured—my husband's illness, times of personal pain, disappointments, people who have backstabbed us and hurt us, and loss of valued relationships, all just temporary afflictions—I can now write this book of poems. God has transformed my storms of life into inspiration for you.

I hope you will learn through your journaling to look beyond the storms of life. Get out of the boat. Walk on water, and the next time God allows the storm, clouds, and rain in your life, you will be ready!

FUEL FOR YOUR JOURNEY. There is a blessing in the storm,

Belinda A. L. Bland

DEDICATIONS

This book is dedicated to and in memory of my parents, *Richard and Margie Law*.

I am who I am today because of my parents. I am able to walk this journey because of the love they imparted to me, the examples they were before me with their care and concern for others, and their loving relationship, which they exhibited before myself and my family. But most of all, their example and teachings of a life lived for Christ!

ACKNOWLEDGEMENTS

To my husband, Raymond. On that day in 2012 when we were told you had Multiple Sclerosis my love for you grew even deeper, and I was reminded of the vow we took on June 7, 2003: "in sickness and in health." I remember the day we embraced this slogan: "I might have MS, but MS will never have me!" I love you with all my heart!

To my wonderful family, I thank you for your unwavering support, prayers and love. Your encouragement helped us to hold on to our faith. I love all of you very much. #LoveMyFamily

THE PROMISE REVEALED

God promised me you some time ago.
We waited patiently
While He pruned and prepared us for each other,
Although it was some time ago.
We allowed God to use us,
For I asked for this some time ago.
Being used of God can be a hurting thing,
And sometimes hard to let Him take full control,
But we relinquished that control,
For we realized some time ago
Our relationship was not of our own,
But was a gift from God,
Who has and will be
Our focus, center and control.
We believed what He told us,
And we stood on what He promised us.
That is why this appointed day,
We stand here together on the promise.
For those of you waiting on a promise from God,
Continue to stand on the promise,
No matter what it looks like,
No matter how it feels,
For the promise shall one day be revealed.

Fuel For Your Journey:
TRUST IN THE LORD WITH ALL THINE HEART.

Look at the following Scriptures and identify the promises of God you see in Isaiah 43:2, 54:10, 54:17, and 2 Peter 1:1-4 Reflect & Journal

_____

_____

_____

_____

_____

_____

_____

_____

_____

_____

_____

_____

_____

_____

_____

YOU ARE MY VESSEL

You are a vessel, wide open to be used of the Lord.
You are a vessel, wide open for My love to
be poured.
You are a vessel, wide open for the world to see
your light.
You are a vessel, wide open for My plans to
take flight.
You are a vessel, wide open for My will to
be seen.
You are a vessel, wide open for My Word to
become a plan
for those who don't understand.
You are a vessel, wide open that I desire to fill
with My love, joy, wisdom, character,
please don't turn a deaf ear.
For your deaf ear can lead to someone else dying,
for you see, without you, they may never hear.
You are My vessel, and extension of Me.
Let's help others together experience
the awesome victory!

Fuel For Your Journey:
GOD NEEDS TO USE YOU.

Think of one way God used you as His vessel during your storm. *Reflect & Journal*

_____

_____

_____

_____

_____

_____

_____

_____

_____

_____

_____

_____

_____

_____

_____

THANK GOD FOR THE STORM

God's hand is upon me.
His love is all around me.
His joy is in me.
His Word speaks through me.
His peace surrounds me.
His grace has seen me through,
For this storm was a storm
That has made me brand new.

Fuel For Your Journey:
LOOK BEYOND THE STORM; HE IS MAKING YOU BRAND NEW.

During the midst of your storm, you may not feel like praising and worshipping God when the pain, disappointment, fear, and anxiety are great. But you must! It is important that you continue to give God praise and worship your way through.

How was your worship as you were going through your storm? Reflect & Journal

_____

_____

_____

_____

_____

_____

_____

_____

_____

_____

_____

_____

_____

_____

_____

_____

_____

_____

_____

Noah did not rely on what he could see; he relied on hearing from the Lord, which he could do because of their intimate relationship.

Noah is a great example for us. He learned the importance of worshipping the Lord. The first act he did after exiting the ark after the flood was an act of worship.

EARLY IN THE MORNING, I RISE

Early in the morning, I rise,

For my soul does not rest.

Early in the morning, I rise;

It stirs as if it were in distress.

But no, it cannot be, for peace is upon my breast.

Early in the morning, I rise,

For my spirit longs to become one with Thee,

Early in the morning, I rise,

For my spirit has allowed God's will to empower me.

Early in the morning, I rise,

For our spirits shall touch and agree.

For today not my will, Lord,

But Your will has become a testimony for me.

Fuel For Your Journey:
YOU WILL HAVE A TESTIMONY TO BE TOLD.

Spiritual preparedness will help you to endure the storm with strength and grace. It will help you to gain greater strength in the aftermath. It is not the burdens of life that weigh us down; it's what we use to handle them. I have learned when we don't know who God is, we don't draw from Him properly. Jesus is the One who gives strength in the midst of your storm.

How spiritually prepared were you during the storm? Reflect & Journal

_____

_____

_____

_____

_____

_____

_____

_____

God's will for you is not always rain-free. Equip yourself with the right physical gear, rain coat, and rain boots. Some of us like rain hats; as for me, I use an umbrella. Spiritually equip yourself with hiding the Word of God in your heart. Stay encouraged, because Jesus is with you. Be ready to get out of the boat; this shows your faith. Keep your eyes on Jesus. Don't doubt and continue to give praise...Your storm will end at the command of Jesus. "Peace, be still."

Call on the name of Jesus, as His Spirit is always with you and He calms down the storms of life.

WHERE ARE YOU, LORD?

Do You hear me, Lord?
Do You see me, Lord?
Can You help me, Lord?
Where are You, Lord?
I'm hurting, Lord…*I'm right here.*
I don't feel You, Lord…*I'm right here.*
I'm lonely, Lord…but *I'm right here.*
My mind won't let me rest…*but I'm here.*
My life is in distress…*I'm right here.*
How much longer, Lord…*Until the lesson is met.*

Fuel For Your Journey:
KNOW THAT GOD WILL NEVER LEAVE YOU.

During your storm, how many times did you ask, "Why me, God?" Did you ever think "Why not you?"
Reflect & Journal

_____

_____

_____

_____

_____

_____

_____

_____

_____

_____

_____

_____

_____

_____

_____

God's timing is not our timing.

God sometimes answers — *yes*, *no*, or *wait*.

During the storm, sometimes God does not speak, but think back on what He may have spoken to you before the storm began. Pay attention to those He used to speak into your life or to your situation.

In the book of Genesis, there is no mention of God speaking to Noah once He shut him and his family in the ark. It takes eyes of faith and strength from within, and sometimes the support of others closest to you, to see God's hand at work in our lives, even when it seems God is silent. In fact, God didn't speak to Noah again until Genesis 8:15, after being shut in the ark. How would you hold up under such a move of God? This *test* became Noah's *testimony*.

What we can learn from the story of Noah is that he had faith, he had strength, and he was at peace; after all, faith is not faith if we know all the details, right? Read this passage from the book of Romans out loud and meditate on what it reveals to you. When God's word is revealed to you if you allow it will shift your mindset:

By entering through faith into what God has always wanted to do for us—set us right with him, make us fit for him—we have it all together with God because of our Master Jesus. And that's not all: We throw open our doors to God and discover at the same moment that he has already thrown open his door to us. We find ourselves standing where we always hoped we might stand—out in the wide-open spaces of God's grace and glory, standing tall and shouting our praise.

There's more to come: We continue to shout our praise even when we're hemmed in with troubles, because we know how troubles can develop passionate patience in us, and how that patience in turn forges the tempered steel of virtue, keeping us alert for whatever God will do next. In alert expectancy such as this, we're never left feeling shortchanged. Quite the contrary—we can't round up enough containers to hold everything God generously pours into our lives through the Holy Spirit! **(Romans 5:1-5)**

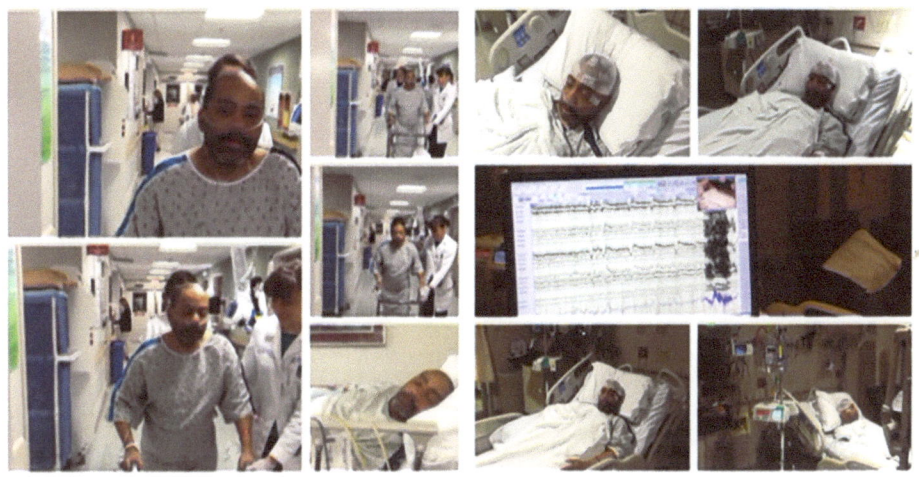

Job was a faithful follower of God before his storm (Job 1:1), but he did not really know God until he had weathered the storm of his life.

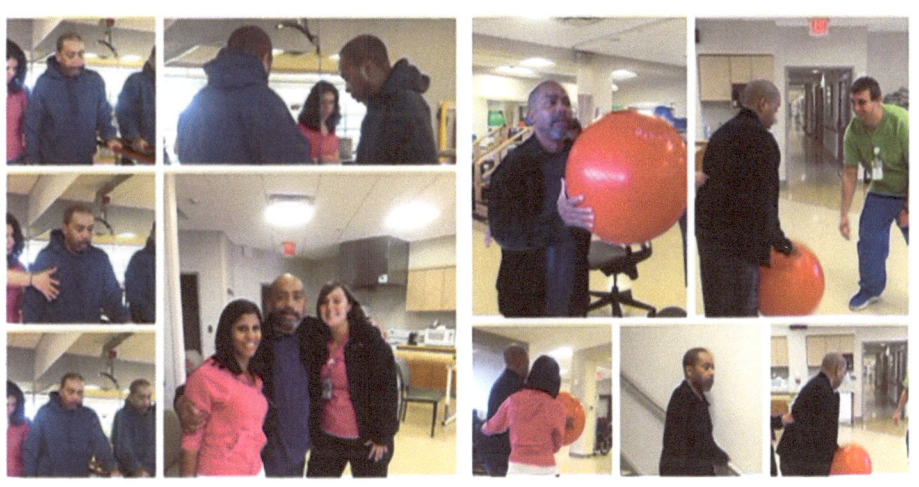

It was then that Job said,
   "My ears had heard of you but now my eyes have seen you."

Job 42:5 (NIV)

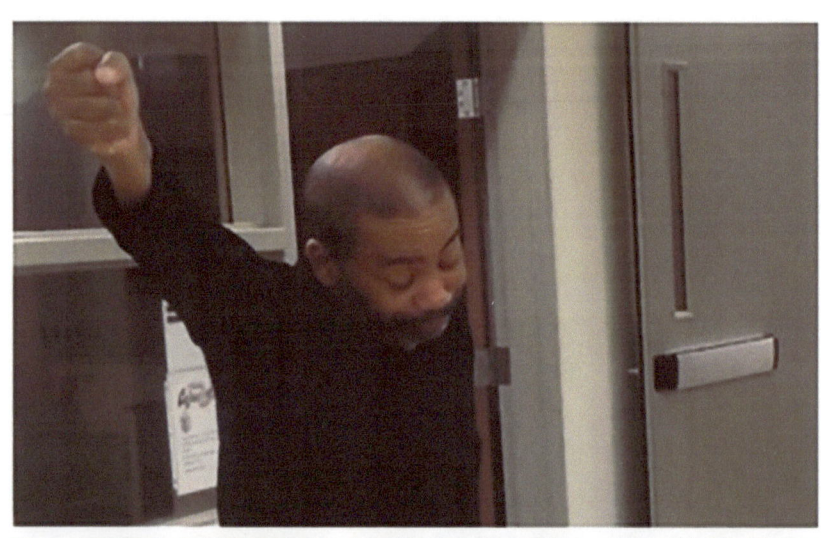

A BLESSING IN DUE TIME

Time is not an issue
when your trust is in the Lord.
Time is not a problem
because God's Word speaks forever more.
Time is not a factor
when we keep our focus on Him.
Time is not a worry
when you walk a path that leads to Him.
But time becomes an
issue, a problem, a factor, a worry
when you turn away from Him.
So keep your eye on the King,
For He is your everything,
and watch His plan in time unfold
And give birth to a testimony to be told.

Fuel For Your Journey:
KNOW THAT YOUR BLESSING IS ON THE WAY.

Did the storm lead you to a closer relationship with Christ? How? *Reflect & Journal*

_____

_____

_____

_____

_____

_____

_____

_____

_____

_____

_____

_____

_____

YOU'RE LOOKING FOR A MIRACLE

You're looking for a miracle,
My child, just wait and see.
The miracle is in store for you,
Just gaze your eyes on Me.
As the new year is approaching,
Your hopes and dreams shall take flight,
For just like the miracle of the virgin birth,
The miracle of your heart's desire
shall soon appear,
Just like that Christmas night.

Fuel For Your Journey:
START PRAISING HIM IN ADVANCE — TO GOD BE THE GLORY!

Name one miracle you have seen God do in your life or someone else's life. *Reflect & Journal*

_____

_____

_____

_____

_____

_____

_____

_____

_____

_____

_____

_____

_____

_____

_____

_____

SPEAK TO YOUR MOUNTAIN – IT'S ONLY A DELAY

Today my blessing was placed on delay,

A promise God made me, so I know it will soon be ok.

There is something that came up against me that has only gotten in the way,

Which I know will be moved

When my God says,

"It's time to reap your blessing; mountain, get out of My child's way."

You see, my faith has become stronger; my focus is fixed on You.

I'm standing on solid ground, and there is no way I will be moved.

This delay is supposed to concern me, move me, and make me doubt You,

And yes, it might have, if I did not trust You.

But this blessing for me has roots that are now full grown, and the due date of arrival, my God,

I know You only know.

But arrival time shall not be a concern of mine, for it shall all be fulfilled in a matter of time.

But something I realized: the closer the blessing,
the more confusion, hurt, and rejecting,

So as I go on with my day, giving God the praise
for allowing this delay,

I thank You, Lord, because I realize I am much
closer now, and I know You are right by my side.

Yes, today my blessing was placed on delay, but
soon You will bless me in Your own special way.

Fuel For Your Journey:
DON'T' BE IN DISMAY – IT'S ONLY A DELAY.

Now that the storm is over, why do you think God allowed the delay (storm) in your life? How did He accomplish His will in your life? What things in you did He perfect?
Reflect & Journal

_____

_____

_____

_____

_____

_____

_____

_____

_____

_____

_____

TODAY SOMEONE ASKED

Today someone asked, "Will you pray with me?"
And you said,
"I'm going through; can you ask someone else to
pray with you?"
And yesterday someone asked, "Can you help me?
And you said,
"I'm going through; I can't be bothered with you."
And one week ago, someone asked,
"Please, do you have a minute to teach me?
And you said,
"I'm going through; can you ask someone else to
teach you? "
A few minutes ago, someone asked,
"Please, I am a little down today; can you
encourage me through?"
And you said,
"I'm a little down too; I'm going through;
I have no strength to encourage you."
Then one day, as you tried to rest,
God called out to you in your distress,
"My child, My child,
even though you are going through,
remember someone else may need you, too.
Just cast your burdens onto Me,
and in the midst of you forgetting
about what you're going through,
I will begin to bless and strengthen you."

Fuel For Your Journey:
GOD CAN MAKE THE BURDENS LIGHT.

As you face the storms of life you are not alone. Rather than focusing on the problems, focus on the promises. Find five Scriptures in the Bible that speak of God's promises regarding burdens.

Reflect & Journal

_____

_____

_____

_____

_____

_____

_____

_____

_____

_____

_____

_____

_____

_____

MY ANEW

I will make this day a day of my Anew

I will start with letting go of the past

and allowing my present to become my Anew

The beginning of my Anew

will start with my attitude

A new look with a new pair of shoes

A new mindset and brand-new hairdo

A new way of living

no more doubting or quitting

A new destiny knowing my worth

and no more pretending

It will be a new way of living

a whole new life with a great new beginning

Today I will make this day my Anew

Fuel For Your Journey:
GOD CAN BRING YOU TO A NEW WAY OF LIVING.

When God starts the rain in your life, He will stop the rain once the rain has done what God intended the storm to do in your life. After the rain from a natural storm, when the sun shines again, there is a freshness in the air. The spiritual storms in your life can bring you to a fresh place and a greater relationship with the Lord, with a different mindset if you allow it, doing just what God intended the storm to do, bringing you to the place where He desired you to be.

The New Oxford American Dictionary defines the word "Anew" as - "in a new way or different and typically more positive way." Fill in the lines below: Because of my Anew I will no longer:

_____

_____

_____

_____

_____

Learn to Look Beyond The Storm

Reflect & Journal

LEARN TO LOOK BEYOND THE STORM

Today you asked me for my hand;
this is a commitment we both understand,
And as I answered you, and I said "I do,"
A rainbow appeared over our heads;
this rainbow was placed in the sky for me
and for you.
This rainbow represents God's covenant,
a covenant between God and me and now you.
This rainbow appeared in the sky;
it followed the lightning, thunder, and darkening
gray skies
This rainbow followed the pouring rain,
but you know –
such a beautiful way to end the pain.
We don't always like to speak of the pain,
but Christ suffered and now He reigns!
Now look what God has birthed in us –
the fruit of His Spirit and an increased trust,
All because we suffered for a while,
went through a few hard trials.
But we made it through the storm
cleansed, refreshed, and now ready to move on.
So our testimony shall always be
learn to look beyond the storm,
For there's a rainbow waiting there
Just for you and for me.

Fuel For Your Journey:
LEARN TO LOOK BEYOND THE STORM.

Journal your journey and then share your story with others ~ Below journal how the test of your storm became your <u>testimony</u>.

Reflect & Journal your story.

_____
_____
_____
_____
_____
_____
_____
_____
_____
_____
_____
_____
_____

PICTURES OF OUR JOURNEY

Learn to Look Beyond The Storm / 35

Learn to Look Beyond The Storm / 37

Reflect & Journal

About the Author

Belinda Bland (Lady Bee), a native Washingtonian and the youngest of three daughters born to the late Margie and Richard Law, is the wife of Pastor Raymond C. Bland.

She was licensed as a minister of the gospel on October 25, 2015. She is a graduate of Howard University with a Bachelor of Science Degree in Psychology and later attended Catholic University of America, where she received her degree as a Registered Nurse.

Lady Bee works joyously beside her husband in ministry at the New Beginnings Christian Life Fellowship Church, in Reading, PA. Together they have raised their daughter, Theresa, and in her later years, one of their goddaughters, Shalynn. She encourages all those whom she comes in contact with to pursue a love relationship with Jesus Christ and enjoy the fullness of God.

COMING SOON!

Learn to Look Beyond the Storm Workbook for small groups.

belindabland.org

Lightning Source UK Ltd.
Milton Keynes UK
UKHW050951101120
373112UK00001B/3